home

home

by David Storey

RANDOM HOUSE · NEW YORK

Library of Congress Catalog Card Number: 74—143996

Manufactured in the United States of America by
The Haddon Craftsmen

2 4 6 8 9 7 5 3

HOME *was first presented on June 17, 1970, by the English Stage Company, at the Royal Court Theatre, London. It was first presented in New York City on November 17, 1970, by Alexander H. Cohen, by arrangement with the English Stage Company, at the Morosco Theatre, with the following cast:*

HARRY	John Gielgud
JACK	Ralph Richardson
MARJORIE	Dandy Nichols
KATHLEEN	Mona Washbourne
ALFRED	Graham Weston

Directed by Lindsay Anderson
Designed by Jocelyn Herbert
Lighting by Jules Fisher
Music by Alan Price
Associate Producer Clinton Wilder
Production Associates Hildy Parks, Roy A. Somlyo
Production Supervisor Jerry Adler

home

Act One
Before lunch

Act Two
After lunch

Act One

SCENE ONE

The stage is bare but for a round metalwork table, set slightly off-center, and two metalwork chairs.

HARRY enters from the right. He is a middle-aged man in his forties. He wears a casual suit, perhaps tweed, with a suitable hat, which, after glancing pleasurably around, he takes off and puts on the table beside him, along with a pair of well-used leather gloves and a folded newspaper.

He presses his shoulders back and eases his neck, making himself comfortable. Then he settles down; he glances at his watch and shakes it to make sure it's going—winding it slowly, looking around.

Stretching his neck again, he leans down and picks out bits of cotton from his trouser cuffs. He examines his shoes, without stooping.

He clears his throat. With his hands clasped in his lap, he gazes out, abstracted, nodding his head slightly, half-smiling.

JACK   Harry!
   (*JACK has come on from the other side. He is dressed in similar fashion, but with a slightly more dandyish flavor: a handkerchief hangs from his top pocket, a rakish trilby is perched on his head. He also has a simple though rather elegant cane*)

HARRY   Jack.

JACK   Been here long?

3

HARRY   No. No.

JACK   Mind?

HARRY   Not at all.
(JACK *sits down. He stretches, showing great relief at being off his feet*)

JACK   Nice to see the sun again.

HARRY   Very.

JACK   Been laid up for a few days.

HARRY   Oh, dear.

JACK   Chill. In bed.

HARRY   Oh, dear. Still . . . Appreciate the comforts.

JACK   What? . . . You're right. Still . . . Nice to be out.

HARRY   'Tis.

JACK   Mind?

HARRY   All yours.
(JACK *picks up the paper and gazes at it without unfolding it*)

JACK   Damn bad news.

HARRY   Yes.

JACK   Not surprising.

HARRY   Gets worse before it gets better.

JACK   S'right . . . Still . . . Not to grumble.

HARRY   No. No.

JACK   Put on a bold front.
  (He turns the paper over)

HARRY   That's right.

JACK   Pretty.
  (He indicates the paper)

HARRY   Very.

JACK   By jove . . . *(Reads intently for a moment)* Oh,
  well.

HARRY   That the one?
  (He glances over)

JACK   *(Nodding)* Yes . . .
  (He clicks his tongue)

HARRY   *(Shaking his head)* Ah, well.

JACK   Yes . . . Still . . .

HARRY   Clouds . . . Watch their different shapes.

JACK   Yes?
  (He looks up at the sky, at which HARRY *is gazing)*

HARRY   See how they drift over?

JACK   By jove.

HARRY   First sight . . . nothing. Then . . . just watch the
  edges . . . See?

JACK   Amazing.

HARRY   Never notice when you're just walking.

5

JACK   No . . . Still . . . best time of the year.

HARRY   What?

Jack   Always think this is the best time.

Harry   Oh, yes.

JACK   Not too hot. Not too cold.

HARRY   Seen that?
(He points at the paper)

JACK   *(Reading for a moment)* By jove . . . *(Reads again briefly)* Well . . . you get some surprises . . . Hello . . . *(Reads further down, turning the edge of the paper over)* Good God!

HARRY   What I felt.

JACK   The human mind.
(He shakes his head)

HARRY   Oh, dear, yes.

JACK   One of these days . . .

HARRY   Ah, yes.

JACK   Then where will they be?

HARRY   Oh, yes.

JACK   Never give it a thought.

HARRY   No . . . Never.

JACK   *(Reading again)* By jove . . . *(He shakes his head. HARRY leans over and removes something casually from JACK's sleeve)*

6

HARRY   Cotton.

JACK   Oh . . . Picked it up . . .
    (He glances around at his other sleeve, then down at his trousers)

HARRY   See you've come prepared.

JACK   What. . . ? Oh. (HARRY *indicates* JACK'*s coat pocket.* JACK *takes out a folded plastic macintosh which is no larger, folded, than his hand)* Best to make sure.

HARRY   Took a risk. Myself.

JACK   Oh, yes . . . What's life worth . . .

HARRY   Oh, yes.

JACK   I say. That was a shock.

HARRY   Yesterday. . . ?

JACK   Bolt from the blue, and no mistake.

HARRY   I'd been half-prepared . . . even then.

JACK   Still a shock.

HARRY   Absolutely.

JACK   My wife . . . you've met? *(Pauses)* Was that last week?

HARRY   Ah, yes.

JACK   Well, a very delicate woman.

HARRY   Still, very sturdy.

JACK   Oh, well. Physically, nothing to complain of.

7

HARRY   Oh, no.

JACK   Temperament, however . . . inclined to the sensitive side.

HARRY   Really?

JACK   Two years ago . . . *(Glances off)* By jove. Isn't that Saxton?

HARRY   Believe it is.

JACK   He's a sharp dresser, and no mistake.

HARRY   Very.

JACK   They tell me . . . Well, I never.

HARRY   Didn't see that, did he? *(They laugh, looking off)* Eyes in the back of your head these days.

JACK   You have. That's right.

HARRY   Won't do that again in a hurry. What?
        (He laughs)

JACK   I had an uncle once who bred horses.

HARRY   Really?

JACK   Used to go down there when I was a boy.

HARRY   The country.

JACK   Nothing like it. What? Fresh air.

HARRY   Clouds.
        (He gestures up)

JACK   I'd say so.

8

HARRY   *My* wife was coming up this morning.

JACK   Really?

HARRY   Slight headache. Thought might be better . . .

JACK   Indoors. Well, best make sure.

HARRY   When I was in the army . . .

JACK   Really? What regiment?

HARRY   Fusiliers.

JACK   Really? How extraordinary.

HARRY   You?

JACK   No, no. A cousin.

HARRY   Well . . .

JACK   Different time, of course.

HARRY   Ah.

JACK   Used to bring his rifle . . . No. That was Arthur.
   Got them muddled.
      (He laughs)

HARRY   Still.

JACK   Never leaves you.

HARRY   No. No.

JACK   In good stead.

HARRY   Oh, yes.

JACK   All your life.

HARRY   Oh, yes.

JACK   I was—for a very short while—in the Royal Air Force.

HARRY   Really?

JACK   Nothing to boast about.

HARRY   Oh, now. Flying?

JACK   On the ground.

HARRY   Chrysanthemums is my wife's hobby.

JACK   Really?

HARRY   Thirty-seven species round the house.

JACK   Beautiful flower.

HARRY   Do you know there are over a hundred?

JACK   Really?

HARRY   Different species.

JACK   Suppose you can mix them up.

HARRY   Oh, very.

JACK   He's coming back . . . (HARRY *looks puzzled*) Swanson.

HARRY   Saxton.

JACK   Saxton! Always did get those two mixed up. Two boys at school: one called Saxton, the other Swanson. Curious thing was, they both looked alike.

HARRY   Really?

JACK   Both had a curious skin disease. Here. Just at the side of the nose.

HARRY   Eczema.

JACK   Really?

HARRY   Could have been.

JACK   Never thought of that . . . When I was young I had an ambition to be a priest, you know.

HARRY   Really?

JACK   Thought about it a great deal.

HARRY   Ah, yes. A great decision.

JACK   Oh, yes.

HARRY   Catholic or Anglican?

JACK   Well . . . Couldn't really make up my mind.

HARRY   Both got a great deal to offer.

JACK   Great deal? My word.

HARRY   Advantages one way. And then . . . in another.

JACK   Oh, yes.

HARRY   One of my first ambitions . . .

JACK   Yes.

HARRY   Oh, now. You'll laugh.

JACK   No. No . . . no. Really.

HARRY   Well . . . I would have liked to have been a
dancer.

JACK   Dancer . . . Tap or "balley"?

HARRY   Oh, well—probably a bit of both.

JACK   A fine thing. Grace.

HARRY   Ah, yes.

JACK   Physical momentum.

HARRY   Yes.

JACK   Swanson might have appreciated that!
(He laughs)

HARRY   Saxton.

JACK   Saxton! By jove . . . At school we had a boy called
Ramsbottom.

HARRY   Really?

JACK   Now, I wouldn't have envied that boy's life.

HARRY   No.

JACK   The euphemisms to which a name . . . well. One
doesn't have to think very far.

HARRY   No.

JACK   A name can be a great embarrassment in life.

HARRY   It can . . . We had—let me think . . . a boy called
Fish.

JACK   Fish!

HARRY And another called Parsons!

JACK Parsons!

HARRY Nicknamed "Nosey."

JACK By jove! *(Laughs; rises)* Some of these nicknames are very clever.

HARRY Yes.

JACK *(Moving away to the right)* I remember, when I was young, I had a very tall friend . . . extremely tall, as a matter of fact. He was called "Lolly."

HARRY Lolly!

JACK It fitted him very well. He . . . *(Distracted, he pauses)* Yes. Had very large teeth as well.

HARRY The past. It conjures up some images.

JACK It does. You're right.

HARRY You wonder how there was ever time for it all.

JACK Time . . . Oh . . . don't mention it.

HARRY A fine cane.

JACK What? Oh that.

HARRY Father had a cane. Walked for miles.

JACK A habit that's fast dying out.

HARRY Oh, yes.

JACK Knew a man, related to a friend of mine, who used to walk twenty miles a day.

HARRY   Twenty!

JACK   Each morning.

HARRY   That really shows some spirit.

JACK   If you keep up a steady pace, you can manage
four miles in the hour.

HARRY   Goodness.

JACK   Five hours. Set off at eight each morning. Back
for lunch at one.

HARRY   Must have had a great appetite.

JACK   Oh, absolutely. Ate like a horse.

HARRY   Stand him in good stead later on.

JACK   Ah, yes . . . Killed, you know. In the war.

HARRY   Oh, dear.

JACK   Funny thing to work out.

HARRY   Oh, yes.

JACK   *(He pauses and sits)*   You do any fighting?

HARRY   What?

JACK   Army.

HARRY   Oh, well, then . . . modest amount.

JACK   Nasty business.

HARRY   Oh! Doesn't bear thinking about.

JACK   Two relatives of mine killed in the war.

HARRY   Oh, dear.

JACK   You have to give thanks, I must say.

HARRY   Oh, yes.

JACK   Mother's father . . . a military man.

HARRY   Yes.

JACK   All his life.

HARRY   He must have seen some sights.

JACK   Oh, yes.

HARRY   Must have all had meaning then.

JACK   Oh, yes. India. Africa. He's buried as a matter of fact in Hong Kong.

HARRY   Really?

JACK   So they tell me. Never been there myself.

HARRY   No.

JACK   Hot climates, I think, can be the very devil if you haven't the temperament.

HARRY   Huh! You don't have to tell me.

JACK   Been there?

HARRY   No, no. Just what one reads.

JACK   Dysentery.

HARRY   Beriberi.

JACK   Yellow fever.

HARRY   Oh, dear.

JACK   . As well, of course, as all the other contingencies.

HARRY   Oh, yes.

JACK   At times one's glad simply to live on an island.

HARRY   Yes.

JACK   Strange that.

HARRY   Yes.

JACK   Without the sea—all around—civilization would never have been the same.

HARRY   Oh, no.

JACK   The ideals of life, liberty, freedom, could never have been the same—democracy—well, if we'd been living on the continent, for example.

HARRY   Absolutely.

JACK   Those your gloves?

HARRY   Yes.

JACK   Got a pair like that at home.

HARRY   Yes?

JACK   Very nearly. The seam goes the other way, I think. *(Picks one up to look)* Yes. It does.

HARRY   A present.

JACK   Really?

HARRY   My wife. At Christmas.

JACK   Season of good cheer.

HARRY   Less and less, of course, these days.

JACK   Oh, my dear man. The whole thing has been ruined. The moment money intrudes . . . all feeling goes straight out of the window.

HARRY   Oh, yes.

JACK   I had an aunt once who owned a little shop.

HARRY   Yes?

JACK   Made almost her entire income during the few weeks before Christmas.

HARRY   Really?

JACK   Never seemed to occur to her that there might be some ethical consideration.

HARRY   Oh, dear.

JACK   Ah, well.

HARRY   Still . . .

JACK   Apart from that, she was a very wonderful person.

HARRY   It's very hard to judge.

JACK   It is.

HARRY   I have a car, for instance.

JACK   Yes?

HARRY One day, in December, I happened to knock a pedestrian over in the street.

JACK Oh, dear.

HARRY It was extremely crowded.

JACK You don't have to tell me. I've seen them.

HARRY Happened to see something they wanted the other side. Dashed across. Before you know where you are . . .

JACK Not serious, I hope?

HARRY No. No. No. Fractured arm.

JACK From that, you know, they might learn a certain lesson.

HARRY Oh, yes.

JACK Experience is a stern master.

HARRY Ah, yes. But then . . .

JACK Perhaps the only one.

HARRY It is.

JACK I had a cousin, on my mother's side, who once fell off a cliff.

HARRY Really?

JACK Quite a considerable height.

HARRY Ah, yes.

JACK   Fell into the sea, fortunately. Dazed. Apart from that, quite quickly recovered.

HARRY   Very fortunate.

JACK   Did it for a dare. Only twelve years old at the time.

HARRY   I remember I fell off a cliff, one time.

JACK   Oh, dear.

HARRY   Not very high. And there was someone there to catch me.
    (He laughs)

JACK   They can be very exciting places.

HARRY   Oh, very.

JACK   I remember I once owned a little boat.

HARRY   Really?

JACK   For fishing. Nothing very grand.

HARRY   A fishing man.

JACK   Not really. More an occasional pursuit.

HARRY   I've always been curious about that.

JACK   Yes?

HARRY   "A solitary figure crouched upon a bank."

JACK   Never stirring.

HARRY   No. No.

JACK   Can be very tedious, I know.

HARRY   Still, a boat is more interesting.

JACK   Oh, yes. A sort of tradition, really.

HARRY   In the family.

JACK   No. No. More in the . . . island, you know.

HARRY   Ah, yes.

JACK   Drake.

HARRY   Yes!

JACK   Nelson.

HARRY   Beatty.

JACK   Sir Walter Raleigh.

HARRY   *There* was a very fine man . . . poet.

JACK   Lost his head, you know.

HARRY   It's surprising the amount of dust that collects in so short a space of time.
(He runs his hand lightly over the table)

JACK   It is. *(Looks around)* Spot like this, perhaps, attracts it.

HARRY   Yes . . . *(Pause)* You never became a priest, then?

JACK   No . . . No.

HARRY   Splendid to have a vocation.

JACK 'Tis . . . Something you believe in.

HARRY Oh, yes.

JACK I could never . . . resolve certain difficulties, my-self.

HARRY Yes?

JACK The hows and the wherefores I could under-stand. How we came to be, and His presence, lurking everywhere, you know. But as to the why . . . I could never understand. Seemed a terrible waste of time to me.

HARRY Oh, yes.

JACK Thought it better to leave it to those who didn't mind.

HARRY Ah, yes.

JACK I suppose the same was true about dancing.

HARRY Oh, yes. I remember turning up, for instance, to my first class, only to discover that all the rest of them were girls.

JACK Really?

HARRY Well . . . there are men dancers, I know. Still . . . Took up football after that.

JACK To professional standard, I imagine.

HARRY Oh, no. Just the odd kick around. Joined a team that played in the park on Sunday mornings.

JACK The athletic life has many attractions.

HARRY   It has. It has.

JACK   *(Pausing)*   How long have you been here, then?

HARRY   Oh, a couple of . . . er . . .

JACK   Strange—meeting the other day.

HARRY   Yes.

JACK   On the way back, thought to myself, "What a chance encounter."

HARRY   Yes.

JACK   So rare, these days, to meet someone to whom one can actually talk.

HARRY   I know what you mean.

JACK   One works. One looks around. One meets people. But very little communication actually takes place.

HARRY   Very.

JACK   None at all in most cases!
       (He laughs)

HARRY   Oh, absolutely.

JACK   The agonies and frustrations. I can assure you. In the end one gives up in absolute despair.

HARRY   Oh, yes.
        (He laughs, rising, and looks off)

JACK   Isn't that Parker?
       (He looks off)

HARRY   No . . . N-no . . . Believe his name is Fielding.

JACK   Could have sworn it was Parker.

HARRY   No. Don't think so . . . Parker walks with a limp. Very slight.

JACK   That's Marshall.

HARRY   Really? Then I've got Parker mixed up again. *(He laughs)*

JACK   Did you see the one who came in yesterday?

HARRY   Hendricks.

JACK   Is that his name?

HARRY   I believe that's what I heard.

JACK   He looked a very suspicious character to me. And his wife . . .

HARRY   I would have thought his girl friend.

JACK   Really? Then that makes far more sense . . . I mean, I have great faith in the institution of marriage, as such.

HARRY   Oh, yes.

JACK   But one thing I've always noticed. When you find a married couple who display their affection in public, then that's an infallible sign that that marriage is breaking up.

HARRY   Really?

JACK   It's a very curious thing. I'm sure there must be some psychological explanation for it.

HARRY   Insecurity.

JACK   Oh, yes.

HARRY   Quite frequently one can judge people entirely by their behavior.

JACK   You can. I believe you're right.

HARRY   Take my father, for instance.

JACK   Oh, yes.

HARRY   An extraordinary man in his own right. And yet, throughout his life he could never put out a light.

JACK   Really?

HARRY   Superstition. If he had to turn off a switch, he'd ask someone else to do it.

JACK   How extraordinary.

HARRY   Quite casually. One never noticed. Over the years one got quite used to it, of course. As a man he was extremely polite.

JACK   Ah, yes.

HARRY   *(He sits)*   Mother, now—she was quite the reverse.

JACK   Oh, yes.

HARRY   Great appetite for life.

JACK   Really?

HARRY   Three.

JACK   Three?

HARRY   Children.

JACK   Ah, yes.

HARRY   Youngest.

JACK   You were?

HARRY   Oh, yes.

JACK   One of seven.

HARRY   Seven!

JACK   Large families in those days.

HARRY   Oh, yes.

JACK   Family life.

HARRY   Oh, yes.

JACK   Society . . . well, without it, wouldn't be what it's like today.

HARRY   Oh, no.

JACK   Still.

HARRY   Ah, yes.

JACK   We have a wonderful example.

HARRY   Oh, my word.

JACK   At times, I don't know where some of us would be without it.

HARRY   No. Not at all.

JACK   A friend of mine—actually, more of an acquaint-
ance, really—was introduced to George the Sixth at
Waterloo.

HARRY   Waterloo?

JACK   The station.

HARRY   By jove.

JACK   He was an assistant to the station master at the
time, in a lowly capacity, of course. His Majesty was
making a weekend trip into the country.

HARRY   Probably to Windsor.

JACK   *(Pausing)*   Can you get to Windsor from Waterloo?

HARRY   I'm . . . No. I'm not sure.

JACK   Sandringham, of course, is in the country.

HARRY   The other way.

JACK   The other way.

HARRY   Balmoral in the Highlands.

JACK   I had an aunt once who, for a short while, lived
near Gloucester.

HARRY   That's a remarkable stretch of the country.

JACK   Vale of Evesham.

HARRY   Vale of Evesham.

JACK   Local legend has it that Adam and Eve originated
there.

HARRY Really?

JACK Has very wide currency, I believe, in the district. For instance, you may have read that portion in the Bible . . .

HARRY I have.

JACK The profusion of vegetation, for example, would indicate that it couldn't, for instance, be anywhere in the Middle East.

HARRY No. No.

JACK On the other hand, the profusion of animals— snakes, for example—would indicate that it might easily be a more tropical environment, as opposed, that is, to one which is merely temperate.

HARRY Yes . . . I see.

JACK Then again, there is ample evidence to suggest that during the period in question equatorial conditions prevailed in the very region in which we are now sitting.

HARRY Really?
    (He looks around)

JACK Discoveries have been made that would indicate that lions and tigers, elephants, wolves, rhinoceros, and so forth, actually inhabited these parts.

HARRY My word.

JACK In those circumstances, it wouldn't be unreasonable to suppose that the Vale of Evesham was such a place itself. The very cradle, as it were, of . . .

HARRY   Close to where your aunt lived.

JACK   That's right.

HARRY   Mind if I have a look?

JACK   Not at all. (HARRY *takes the cane*)

HARRY   You seldom see canes of this quality these days.

JACK   No. No. That's right.

HARRY   I believe they've gone out of fashion.

JACK   They have.

HARRY   Like beards.

JACK   Beards!

HARRY   My father had a small mustache.

JACK   A mustache, I've always thought, became a man.

HARRY   Chamberlain.

JACK   Roosevelt.

HARRY   Schweitzer.

JACK   Chaplin.

HARRY   Hitler . . .

JACK   Travel, I've always felt, was a great broadener of the mind.

HARRY   My word.

JACK   Traveled a great deal—when I was young.

HARRY Far?

JACK Oh, all over.

HARRY A great thing.

JACK Sets its mark upon a man.

HARRY Like the army.

JACK Like the army. I suppose the fighting you do has very much the same effect.

HARRY Oh, yes.

JACK Bayonet?

HARRY What?

JACK The . . . er . . .

HARRY Oh, bayonet . . . ball and flame. The old three, as we used to call them.

JACK Ah, yes.

HARRY A great welder of character.

JACK By jove.

HARRY The youth of today: might have done some good.

JACK Oh, my word, yes.

HARRY In the Royal Air Force, of course . . .

JACK Bombs.

HARRY Really.

JACK   Cannon.

HARRY   Ah, yes . . . Couldn't have got far, in our job, I can tell you, without the Royal Air Force.

JACK   No. No.

HARRY   Britannia rules the waves . . . and rules the skies, too, I shouldn't wonder.

JACK   Oh, yes.

HARRY   Nowadays, of course . . .

JACK   Rockets.

HARRY   Ah, yes.

JACK   They say . . .

HARRY   Yes?

JACK   When the next catastrophe occurs . . .

HARRY   Oh, yes.

JACK   That the island itself might very well be flooded.

HARRY   Really?

JACK   Except for the more prominent peaks, of course.

HARRY   Oh, yes.

JACK   While we're sitting here waiting to be buried . . .

HARRY   Oh, yes.

JACK   *(Laughing)*   We'll end up being drowned.

HARRY   Extraordinary! *(Laughs)* No Vale of Evesham then.

JACK   Oh, no.

HARRY   Nor your aunt at Gloucester!

JACK   She died a little while ago, you know.

HARRY   Oh, I am sorry.

JACK   We weren't very attached.

HARRY   Oh, no.

JACK   Still, she was a very remarkable woman.

HARRY   Ah, yes.

JACK   In her own particular way. So few characters around these days. So few interesting people.

HARRY   Oh, yes.

JACK   Uniformity.

HARRY   Mrs. Washington.
      (He looks off)

JACK   Really? I've been keeping an eye open for her.

HARRY   Striking woman.

JACK   Her husband was related to a distant cousin of mine, on my father's side.

HARRY   My word.

JACK   I shouldn't be surprised if she recognizes me . . . No . . .

HARRY   Scarcely glanced. Her mind on other things.

JACK   Oh, yes.
        (There is a long silence)

HARRY   Spot of cloud there.

JACK   Ever seen this? *(Takes out a coin)* There. Nothing
up my sleeve. Ready? One, two, three . . . Gone.

HARRY   My word.

JACK   Here . . . *(Takes out three cards)* Pick out the
Queen of Hearts.

HARRY   This one.

JACK   That's right . . . Now . . . Queen of Hearts.

HARRY   This one.

JACK   No!

HARRY   Oh!
        (They laugh)

JACK   Try again . . . There she is. *(Shuffles them around
on the table)* Where is she?

HARRY   Er . . .

JACK   Take your time.

HARRY   This one . . . Oh!
        (They laugh)

JACK   That one!

HARRY   Well, I'll have to study those.

JACK Easy when you know how. I have some more
back there. One of my favorite tricks is to take the ace
of spades out of someone's top pocket.

HARRY Oh . . .
(He looks)

JACK No, no, no. *(Laughs)* It needs some preparation
. . . Sometimes in a lady's handbag. That goes down
very well.

HARRY Goodness.

JACK I knew a man at one time—a friend of the family,
on my father's side—who could put a lighted ciga-
rette into his mouth, take one half from one ear, and
the other half from the other.

HARRY Goodness.

JACK Still lighted.

HARRY How on earth did he do that?

JACK I don't know.

HARRY I suppose—physiologically—it's possible, then.

JACK Shouldn't think so.

HARRY No.

JACK One of the advantages, of course, of sitting here.

HARRY Oh, yes.

JACK You can see everyone walking past.

HARRY Oh, yes.

JACK Jennings isn't a man I'm awfully fond of.

HARRY No.

JACK You've probably noticed yourself.

HARRY I have. In the army, I met a man . . . Private
. . . er . . .

JACK The equivalent rank, of course, in the Air Force,
is aircraftsman.

HARRY Or able seaman. In the navy.

JACK Able seaman.
(They laugh)

HARRY Goodness.

JACK Funny name. *(Laughs)* Able seaman. I don't
think I'd like to be called that.

HARRY Yes!
(He laughs)

JACK Able seaman! *(Snorts)* One of the great things, of
course, about the war, was its feeling of camaraderie.

HARRY Friendship.

JACK You found that too? On the airfield where I was
stationed it was really like one great big happy family.
My word, the things one did for one another.

HARRY Oh, yes.

JACK The way one worked.

HARRY Soon passed.

JACK Oh, yes. It did. It did.

HARRY Ah, yes.

JACK No sooner was the fighting over than back it came. Backbiting. Complaints. Getting what you can. I sometimes think if the war had been prolonged another thirty years we'd have all felt the benefit.

HARRY Oh, yes.

JACK One's children would have grown up far different, that's for sure.

HARRY Really? How many have you got?

JACK Two.

HARRY Oh, that's very nice.

JACK Boy married. Girl likewise. They seem to rush into things so early these days.

HARRY Oh, yes.

JACK And you?

HARRY Oh, no. No. Never had the privilege.

JACK Ah, yes. Responsibility. At times you wonder if it's worth it. I had a cousin, on my father's side, who threw herself from a railway carriage.

HARRY Oh, dear. How awful.

JACK Yes.

HARRY Killed outright.

JACK Well, fortunately, it had just pulled into a station.

HARRY   I see.

JACK   Daughter's married to a salesman. Refrigerators; he sells appliances of that nature.

HARRY   Oh. Opposite to me.

JACK   Yes?

HARRY   Heating engineer.

JACK   Really? I'd never have guessed. How extraordinary.

HARRY   And yourself.

JACK   Oh, I've tinkered with one or two things.

HARRY   Ah, yes.

JACK   What I like about my present job is the scope that it leaves you for initiative.

HARRY   Rather. Same with mine.

JACK   Distribution of foodstuffs in a wholesale store.

HARRY   Really?

JACK   Thinking out new ideas. Constant speculation.

HARRY   Oh, yes.

JACK   Did you know if you put jam into small cardboard containers it will sell far better than if you put it into large glass jars?

HARRY   Really?

JACK   Psychological. When you buy it in a jar you're

wondering what on earth—subconsciously—you're going to do with the glass bottle. But with a cardboard box that anxiety is instantly removed. Result: improved sales, improved production, lower prices, improved distribution.

HARRY   That's a fascinating job.

JACK   Oh, yes. If you use your brains there's absolutely nothing there to stop you.

HARRY   I can see.

JACK   Heating must be a very similar problem.

HARRY   Oh, yes.

JACK   The different ways of warming up a house.

HARRY   Yes.

JACK   Or not warming it up, as the case may be.

HARRY   Yes!
     (They laugh)

JACK   I don't think I've met your wife.

HARRY   No. No . . . As a matter of fact, we've been separated for a little while.

JACK   Oh, dear.

HARRY   One of those misfortunes.

JACK   Happens a great deal.

HARRY   Oh, yes.

JACK   Each have our cross.

HARRY   Oh, yes.

JACK   Well, soon be time for lunch.

HARRY   Will. And I haven't had my walk.

JACK   No. Still . . .

HARRY   Probably do as much good.

JACK   Oh, yes.

HARRY   Well, then . . .
        (He stretches and gets up)

JACK   Yours or mine?

HARRY   Mine . . . I believe.
        (He picks up the newspaper)

JACK   Ah, yes.

HARRY   Very fine gloves.

JACK   Yes.

HARRY   Pacamac.

JACK   All correct.

HARRY   Cane.

JACK   Cane.

HARRY   Well, then. Off we go.

JACK   Off we go.
        (HARRY *breathes in deeply, then breathes out*)

HARRY   Beautiful corner.

JACK   'Tis.
       (They pause and take a last look around)

HARRY   Work up an appetite.

JACK   Right, then. Best foot forward.

HARRY   Best foot forward.

JACK   Best foot forward, and off we go.
       (They stroll off, taking the air)

SCENE TWO

KATHLEEN *and* MARJORIE *enter.*

KATHLEEN *is a stout, middle-aged lady; she wears a coat, which is unbuttoned, a headscarf, and strap shoes. She is limping, her arm supported by* MARJORIE.

MARJORIE *is also middle-aged. She is dressed in a skirt and cardigan. She carries an umbrella and a large, well-used bag.*

KATHLEEN   Cor . . . *blimey!*

MARJORIE   Going to rain, ask me.

KATHLEEN   Rain all it wants, ask me. Cor . . . *blimey!* Going to kill me, is this.
(She limps to a chair, sits down and holds her foot)

MARJORIE   Going to rain and catch us out here. That's what it's going to do.
(She puts her umbrella up; it is worn, but not excessively so)

KATHLEEN   Going to rain, all right, in't it? Going to rain, all right . . . Put your umbrella up—sun's still shining. Cor blimey. Invite rain, that will. Common sense, girl . . . Cor *blimey* . . . My bleedin' feet . . .
(She rubs one foot without removing her shoe)

MARJORIE   Out here and no shelter. Be all right if it starts.

(She moves her umbrella one way, then another, looking up)

KATHLEEN Cor blimey . . . Surprise me they don't drop off . . . Cut clean through, these will.

MARJORIE *(Looking skywards, however)* Clouds all over. Told you we shouldn't have come out.

KATHLEEN Get nothing if you don't try, girl . . . Cor *blimey!*
(She winces)

MARJORIE I don't know.

KATHLEEN Here. You'll be all right, won't you? (MAR-JORIE *looks puzzled*) Holes, there is. See right through, you can.

MARJORIE What?

KATHLEEN Here. Rain come straight through that. Won't get much shelter under that. What d'I tell you? Might as well sit under a shower. *(Laughs)* Cor blimey. You'll be all right, won't you?

MARJORIE Be all right with you in any case. Walk no faster than a snail.

KATHLEEN Not suprised. Don't want me to escape. That's my trouble, girl.

MARJORIE Here . . .
(JACK and HARRY slowly pass upstage, taking the air, chatting. MARJORIE and KATHLEEN wait for them to pass)

KATHLEEN What've we got for lunch?

4 I

MARJORIE   Sprouts.

KATHLEEN   *(Massaging her foot)*   Seen them, have you?

MARJORIE   Smelled 'em!

KATHLEEN   What's today, then?

MARJORIE   Friday.

KATHLEEN   End of week.

MARJORIE   Corn' beef hash.

KATHLEEN   That's Wednesday.

MARJORIE   Sausage roll.

KATHLEEN   Think you're right . . . Cor *blimey*.
(She groans, holding her foot)

MARJORIE   Know what you ought to do, don't you?
(KATHLEEN *groans, holding her foot*) Ask for another
pair of shoes, girl, you ask me.

KATHLEEN   Took me laced ones, haven't they? Only
ones that fitted. Thought I'd hang myself, didn't
they? Only five inches long.

MARJORIE   What they think you are?

KATHLEEN   Bleedin' mouse, more likely.

MARJORIE   Here. Not like the last one I was in.

KATHLEEN   No?

MARJORIE   Let you paint on the walls, they did. Do
anyfing. Just muck around . . . Here . . . I won't tell
you what some of them did.

KATHLEEN   What? (MARJORIE *leans over and whispers*) Never.

MARJORIE   Cross me heart.

KATHLEEN   Glad I wasn't there. This place is bad enough. You seen Henderson, have you?

MARJORIE   Ought to lock him up, you ask me.

KATHLEEN   What d'you do, then?

MARJORIE   Here?

KATHLEEN   At this other place.

MARJORIE   Noffing. Mucked around . . .

KATHLEEN   Here . . .
         (JACK *and* HARRY *stroll back again slowly, in conversation, with their heads back, breathing deeply, bracing arms* . . . MARJORIE *and* KATHLEEN *wait till they pass*)

MARJORIE   My dentist comes from Pakistan.

KATHLEEN   Yours?

MARJORIE   Took out all me teeth.

KATHLEEN   Those not your own, then?

MARJORIE   All went rotten when I had my little girl. There she is, waitress at the seaside.

KATHLEEN   And you stuck here . . .

MARJORIE   No teeth . . .

KATHLEEN   Don't appreciate it.

MARJORIE They don't.

KATHLEEN Never.

MARJORIE Might take this down if it doesn't rain.

KATHLEEN Cor blimey . . . take these off if I thought I
could get 'em on again . . . *(Groans)* Tried catching a
serious disease.

MARJORIE When was that?

KATHLEEN Only had me in two days. Said, Nothing
the matter with you, my girl.

MARJORIE Don't believe you.

KATHLEEN Next thing—got home; smashed everything in sight.

MARJORIE No?

KATHLEEN Winders. Cooker . . . Nearly broke me back
. . . Thought I'd save the telly. Still owed eighteen
months. Thought: Everything or nothing, girl.

MARJORIE Rotten programs.

KATHLEEN Didn't half give it a good old conk.

MARJORIE *(Looking around)* There's one thing. You
get a good night's sleep.

KATHLEEN Like being with a steam engine, where I
come from. Cor blimey, that much whistling and
groaning; think you're going to take off.

MARJORIE More like a boa constrictor, ask me. Here
. . . (JACK *and* HARRY *stroll back, still taking the air;*

bracing arms, heads back) Started crying everywhere I went . . . Started off on Christmas Eve.

KATHLEEN S'happy time, Christmas.

MARJORIE Didn't stop till Boxing Day.

KATHLEEN If He ever comes again, I hope He comes on Whit Tuesday. For me that's the best time of the year.

MARJORIE Why's that?

KATHLEEN Dunno. Whit Tuesday's always been a lucky day for me. First party I ever went to was on a Whit Tuesday. First feller I went with. Can't be the date. Different every year.

MARJORIE My lucky day's the last Friday in any month with an "r" in it when the next month doesn't begin later than the following Monday.

KATHLEEN How do you make that out?

MARJORIE Dunno. I was telling the doctor that the other day . . . There's that man with the binoculars watching you.

KATHLEEN Where?

MARJORIE Lift your dress up.

KATHLEEN No.

MARJORIE Go on . . . *(She leans over and does it for her)* . . . Told you . . .

KATHLEEN Looks like he's got diarrhea! *(They laugh)*

4 5

See that chap the other day? Showed his slides of a trip up the Amazon River.

MARJORIE   See that one with no clothes on? Supposed to be cooking his dinner.

KATHLEEN   Won't have him here again . . .

MARJORIE   Showing all his p's and q's.

KATHLEEN   Oooooh!
(She laughs, covering her mouth)

MARJORIE   Here . . .
(JACK and HARRY stroll back, a little closer, this time, to MARJORIE and KATHLEEN, and glance over now at them)

KATHLEEN   Lord and Lady used to live here at one time.

MARJORIE   Who's that?

KATHLEEN   Dunno.

MARJORIE   Probably still inside, ask me . . . *(Glances after JACK and HARRY as they stroll off)* See that woman with dyed hair? Told me she'd been in films. "What films?" I said. "Blue films?"

KATHLEEN   What she say?

MARJORIE   "The ones I was in was not in color." *(They laugh)* I sh'll lose me teeth one of these days . . . oooh!

KATHLEEN   Better 'n losing something else . . .

MARJORIE   Ooooh!
(They laugh again)

4 6

KATHLEEN Here . . .
(JACK *and* HARRY *have strolled back on*)

JACK *(Removing his hat)* Good day, ladies.

KATHLEEN Good day yourself, your lordships.

JACK Oh, now. I wouldn't go as far as that.
(*He laughs politely and looks at* HARRY)

HARRY No. No. Still a bit of the common touch.

JACK Least, so I'd hope.

HARRY Oh, yes.

MARJORIE And how have you been keeping, Professor?

JACK Professor? I can see we're a little elevated today.

MARJORIE Don't know about elevated. But *we're* sitting
down.
(KATHLEEN *and* MARJORIE *laugh*)

KATHLEEN Been standing up, we have, for hours.

HARRY Hours?

MARJORIE When you were sitting down.

JACK Oh, dear . . . I wasn't aware . . .

KATHLEEN 'Course you were. My bleedin' feet. Just
look at them.
(She holds them again)

MARJORIE Pull your skirt down, girl.

KATHLEEN Oh, Gawd . . .

JACK   My friend here, Harry, is a specialist in house-warming, and I myself am a retailer in preserves.

MARJORIE   Ooooh! (*Screeches, laughs, covering her mouth; then, aside to* KATHLEEN) What did I tell you?

KATHLEEN   No atomic bombs today?

JACK   (*Looking up at the sky behind him*) No, no. Shouldn't think so.

MARJORIE   And how's your mongol sister?

HARRY   Mongol . . . ? I'm afraid you must have the wrong person, ma'am.

KATHLEEN   Ooooh!
(*She screeches, then laughs*)

JACK   My friend, I'm afraid, is separated from his wife. As a consequence, I can assure you, of many hardships . . .

MARJORIE   Of course . . .

JACK   And I myself, though happily married in some respects, would not pretend that my situation is all it should be . . .

KATHLEEN   Ooooh!

JACK   One endeavors . . . but it is in the nature of things, I believe, that, on the whole, one fails.

KATHLEEN   Ooooh!

HARRY   My friend . . . Jack . . . has invented several new methods of retailing jam.

KATHLEEN   Ooooh!

MARJORIE   Jam. I like that.

JACK   Really?

MARJORIE   (*To* KATHLEEN)   Strawberry. My favorite.

KATHLEEN   Raspberry, mine.

MARJORIE   Ooooh!
(KATHLEEN *and* MARJORIE *laugh*)

JACK   A friend of mine, on my father's side, once owned a small factory which was given over, exclusively, to its manufacture.

KATHLEEN   Ooooh!

JACK   In very large vats.

KATHLEEN   Ooooh!

MARJORIE   I like treacle, myself.

JACK   Treacle, now, is a very different matter.

MARJORIE   Comes from Malaya.

HARRY   That's rubber, I believe.

MARJORIE   In tins.

HARRY   The rubber comes from Malaya, I believe.

MARJORIE   I eat it, don't I? I ought to know.

KATHLEEN   She has treacle on her bread.

JACK   I believe it comes, as a matter of fact, from the West Indies.

KATHLEEN   West Indies? Where's that?

MARJORIE   Near Hong Kong.

HARRY   That's the East Indies, I believe.

MARJORIE   You ever been to the North Indies?

HARRY   I don't believe . . .

MARJORIE   Well, that's where treacle comes from.

HARRY   I see . . .
(There is a pause; the tone has suddenly become serious)

JACK   We were just remarking, as a matter of fact, that Mrs. Glover isn't looking her usual self.

KATHLEEN   Who's she?

HARRY   She's . . .

JACK   The lady with the rather embarrassing disfigurement . . .

MARJORIE   Her with one ear?

KATHLEEN   The one who's only half a nose.

MARJORIE   She snores.

KATHLEEN   You'd snore as well, wouldn't you, if you only had half a nose.

MARJORIE   Eaten away.

KATHLEEN What?

MARJORIE Her husband ate it one night when she was sleeping.

KATHLEEN Silly to fall asleep with any man, I say. These days they get up to anything. Read it in the papers, an' next thing they want to try it themselves.

HARRY The weather's been particularly mild today.

KATHLEEN Not like my flaming feet. Oooh . . .

JACK As one grows older these little things are sent to try us.

KATHLEEN Little? Cor blimey; I take size seven.

HARRY My word.

MARJORIE He wishes he was sitting in this chair, doesn't he?

HARRY What . . .

JACK It's extraordinary that more facilities of this nature aren't supplied, in my view.

KATHLEEN Only bit of garden with any flowers. Half a dozen daisies . . .

HARRY Tulips . . .

JACK Roses . . .

KATHLEEN I know daisies, don't I? Those are daisies. Grow three feet tall.

HARRY Really?

MARJORIE   Rest of it's all covered in muck.

JACK   Oh, now. Not as bad as that.

MARJORIE   What? I call that muck. What's it supposed
to be?

HARRY   A rockery, I believe.

KATHLEEN   Rockery? More like a rubbish tip, ask me.

JACK   Probably the flowers haven't grown yet.

MARJORIE   Flowers? How do you grow flowers on old
bricks and bits of plaster?

HARRY   Certain categories, of course . . .

JACK   Oh, yes.

HARRY   Can be trained to grow in these conditions.

KATHLEEN   You're round the bend, you are. Ought to
have you up there, they did.

HARRY   (*To* JACK)   They tell me the flowers are just as
bad at that end, too.
(HARRY *and* JACK *laugh at their private joke*)

MARJORIE   If you ask me, all this is just typical.

JACK   Typical?

MARJORIE   One table; two chairs . . . Between one thousand people.

KATHLEEN   Two, they tell me.

MARJORIE   Two thousand. One thousand for this chair,
and one thousand for that.

HARRY   There are, of course, the various benches.

KATHLEEN   Benches? Seen better sold for firewood.

MARJORIE   Make red marks, they do, across your bum.

KATHLEEN   Ooooh!
(She screeches, covering her mouth)

HARRY   Clouding slightly.

JACK   Slightly.
(He looks up)

MARJORIE   Pull your skirt down, girl.

KATHLEEN   Oooh!

HARRY   Of course, one alternative would be to bring, say, a couple of more chairs out with us.

JACK   Oh, yes. Now that would be a solution.

HARRY   Four chairs. One each. I don't believe, say, for an afternoon they'd be missed from the lecture hall.

MARJORIE   Here, you see *Up the Amazon* last night?

JACK   Tuesday . . .

HARRY   Tuesday.

JACK   Believe I did, now you mention it.

MARJORIE   See that feller with a loincloth?

KATHLEEN   Ooooh!
(She laughs, covering her mouth)

JACK   I must admit, there are certain attractions in the primitive life.

KATHLEEN   Ooooh!

JACK   Air, space . . .

MARJORIE   Seen all he's got, that's all you seen.

JACK   I believe there was a moment when the eye . . .

KATHLEEN   Moment . . . Ooooh!

HARRY   I thought his pancakes looked rather nice.

KATHLEEN   Ooooh!

HARRY   On the little log . . .

KATHLEEN   Ooooh!

MARJORIE   Not his pancakes he's seen, my girl.

KATHLEEN   Ooooh!

JACK   The canoe, now, was not unlike my own little boat.

KATHLEEN   Ooooh!

HARRY   Fishing there somewhat more than a mere pastime.

JACK   Oh, yes.

HARRY   Life and death.

JACK   Oh, yes.

MARJORIE   Were you the feller they caught climbing out of a window here last week?

JACK   Me?

MARJORIE   Him.

HARRY   Don't think so . . . Don't recollect that.

JACK   Where, if you don't mind me asking, did you
acquire that information?

MARJORIE   Where? (*To* KATHLEEN) Here, I thought you
told me it was him.

KATHLEEN   Not me. Mrs. Heller.

MARJORIE   You sure?

KATHLEEN   Not me, anyway.

JACK   I had a relative—nephew, as a matter of fact, who
started a window-cleaning business . . . let me see—
three years ago now.

HARRY   Really?

JACK   Great scope there for an adventurous man.

MARJORIE   In bathroom windows 'specially.

KATHLEEN   Ooooh!

JACK   Heights . . . distances . . .

HARRY   On very tall buildings, of course, they lower
them from the roof.

JACK   Oh, yes.

HARRY   Don't have the ladders long enough, you know.

KATHLEEN   Ooooh!

JACK   Your friend seems in a very jovial frame of mind.

HARRY   Like to see that.

JACK   Oh, yes. Gloom—one sees it far too much in this place. Mr. Metcalf, now, I don't think he's spoken to anyone since the day that he arrived.

MARJORIE   What's he, then?

HARRY   He's the gentleman who's constantly pacing up and down.

JACK   One says hello, of course. He scarcely seems to notice.

KATHLEEN   Hear you were asking if they'd let you out.

JACK   Who?

MARJORIE   Your friend.

HARRY   Oh. Nothing as dramatic . . . certain inquiries, temporary visit . . . Domestic problems, you know. Without a man very little, I'm afraid, gets done.

MARJORIE   It gets too much done, if you ask me. That's half the trouble.

KATHLEEN   Ooooh!

HARRY   However . . . It seems that certain aspects of it can be cleared up by correspondence. One doesn't wish, after all, to impose unduly . . .

JACK   Oh, no.

HARRY   Events have their own momentum. Take their time.

MARJORIE You married to me, they would. I can tell you.

KATHLEEN Ooooh!

HARRY Oh, now . . . Missis . . . er . . .

MARJORIE Madam.

KATHLEEN Ooooh!

HARRY Well . . . er . . . that might be a situation that could well be beneficial to us both, in different circumstances, in different places . . .

JACK Quite . . .

MARJORIE Listen to him!

HARRY We all have our little foibles, our little failings.

JACK Oh, indeed.

HARRY Hardly be human without.

JACK Oh, no.

HARRY The essence of true friendship, in my view, is to make allowances for one another's little lapses.

MARJORIE Heard all about your little lapses, haven't we?

KATHLEEN Ooooooh!

JACK All have our little falls from grace.

MARJORIE Pull your skirt down, girl!

KATHLEEN Ooooooh!

MARJORIE   Burn down the whole bleedin' building, he will. Given up smoking because they won't let him have any matches.

KATHLEEN   Oooh!

JACK   The rumors that drift around a place like this . . . hardly worth the trouble . . .

HARRY   Absolutely.

JACK   If one believed everything one heard . . .

HARRY   Oh, yes.

JACK   I was remarking to my friend earlier this morning: if one can't enjoy life as it takes one, what's the point of living it at all? One can't, after all, spend the whole of one's life inside a shell.

HARRY   Oh, no.

MARJORIE   Know what he'd spend it inside if he had half a chance.

KATHLEEN   Ooooooh!

MARJORIE   Tell my husband of you, I shall.

KATHLEEN   Bus driver.

JACK   Really? I've taken a lifelong interest in public transport.

KATHLEEN   Oooh!

MARJORIE   Taken a lifelong interest in something else more 'n likely.

KATHLEEN   Ooooooh!

MARJORIE   Pull your skirt down, girl!

KATHLEEN   Oooooh!

MARJORIE   Know his kind.

KATHLEEN   Oooooh!

JACK   Respect for the gentler sex, I must say, is a fast
diminishing concept in the modern world.

HARRY   Oh, yes.

JACK   I recollect the time when one stood for a lady as
a matter of course.

HARRY   Oh, yes.

MARJORIE   Know the kind of standing he's on about.

KATHLEEN   Oooooh!

JACK   Each becomes hardened to his ways.

KATHLEEN   Oooooh!

JACK   No regard for anyone else's.

MARJORIE   Be missing your dinner, you will. (*To* JACK)
Here. Are you all right?

JACK   Slight moment of discomposure . . .
(JACK *has begun to cry, vaguely. He takes out a
handkerchief to wipe his eyes*)

HARRY   My friend is a man—he won't mind me saying
this—

59

JACK No . . . no . . .

HARRY Of great sensibility and feeling.

KATHLEEN Here. You having us on?

JACK I assure you, madam . . . I regret any anxiety, or concern which I may, unwittingly, have caused. In fact—I'm sure my friend will concur—perhaps you'll allow us to accompany you to the dining hall. I have noticed, in the past, that though one has to queue, to leave it any later is to run the risk of being served with a cold plate; the food cold, and the manners of the cook—at times, I must confess . . . appalling.

KATHLEEN (*To* MARJORIE) We'll have to go. There'll be nothing left.

MARJORIE It's this seat he's after.

HARRY I assure you, madam . . . we are on our way.

KATHLEEN Here—you mind if I lean on your arm?

MARJORIE Kathleen!

HARRY Oh, now. That's a very pretty name.

KATHLEEN Got straps . . . make your ankles swell.

HARRY Allow me.

KATHLEEN Oh, thank you.

HARRY Harry.

KATHLEEN Harry.

HARRY And this is my friend—Jack.

KATHLEEN Jack . . . And this is my friend Marjorie.

JACK Marjorie . . . Delightful.

MARJORIE (*To* KATHLEEN) Here. You all right?

KATHLEEN You carrying it with you, or are you coming?

JACK Allow me . . .
(*He holds her seat*)

MARJORIE Here . . .
(*She gets up, suspicious*)

JACK (*Pausing*) Marjorie . . .

HARRY Perhaps after lunch we might meet here again.

JACK A little chat . . . Time passes very slowly.

MARJORIE Here, where's my bag?

KATHLEEN Need carrying out, I will.
(HARRY *has taken* KATHLEEN'*s arm*)

HARRY Now, then. All right.

KATHLEEN Have you all the time, I shall.

HARRY Ready? . . . All aboard, then, are we?

MARJORIE Well, then. All right . . .

JACK Right then . . . Dining hall—here we come!
(*They start off slowly;* HARRY *and* KATHLEEN *are in front*)

HARRY Sausages today, if I'm not mistaken.

KATHLEEN   Ooooh!

MARJORIE   Corned beef hash.

KATHLEEN   Ooooh!

JACK   One as good as another, I always say.

KATHLEEN   Oooooh!

HARRY   Turned out better.

JACK   Turned out better.

HARRY   Altogether.

JACK   Altogether.

HARRY   Well, then, here we go.
       (They leave)

Act Two

ALFRED *comes in; he is a well-built young man of about* *thirty. His jacket is unbuttoned; he has no tie.*
He sees the table and walks past it slowly, eying it. He *pauses, and glances back at it. Then he comes back, watching* *the table rather furtively, sideways. He pauses again, with* *his hands behind his back, regarding it.*
Suddenly he moves towards it and grasps it, struggling *with it as if it had a life of its own. He groans and continues* *to struggle, finally lifting the table above his head.*
While he is struggling with it, MARJORIE *enters, as* *before, carrying her furled umbrella.*

MARJORIE   Here. You all right?

ALFRED   What?

MARJORIE   Alfred, i'n it?

ALFRED   Yeh.
         (He is still holding the table above his head)

MARJORIE   You'll break that, you will.

ALFRED   Yeh . . .
         (He looks up at it. MARJORIE, *however, isn't much* *interested; she is already looking around)*

MARJORIE   You seen my mate? (ALFRED *looks puzzled)*
   Woman that limps.

6 5

ALFRED   No.

(ALFRED *pauses before all his answers*)

MARJORIE   One day you get seconds and they go off without you. You like treacle pud'?

ALFRED   Yeh.

MARJORIE   Get seconds?

AFLRED   No.

MARJORIE   Shoulda waited.

ALFRED   Yeh.

MARJORIE   Said they'd be out here after remedials. (AL-FRED *looks at her quizzically*) You do remedials?

ALFRED   Yeh.

MARJORIE   What you do?

ALFRED   Baskets.

MARJORIE   Baskets. Shoulda known.

AFLRED   You got sixpence?

MARJORIE   No. (ALFRED *lifts the table up and down ceremoniously above his head*) Better go find her. Let anybody turn them 'round her hand, she will.

ALFRED   Yeh.

(MARJORIE *leaves.* ALFRED *lowers the table slowly, almost like a ritual. He crouches, picks up one chair by the foot of one leg and lifts it slowly, exaggerating the effort. Then he stands slowly, as he gets it up. He bends his arm slowly, lifting the chair above his*

*head. He puts it down and stands a moment, gazing
down at the two chairs and the table, sideways. He
walks around them, pauses and walks around a little
further. Then he grabs the second chair and lifts it,
one-handed, like the first chair, but more quickly.
Lifting it above his head, he begins to wrestle with
it as if it too possessed a life of its own; his grip,
however, is still one-handed.* MARJORIE *enters,
pauses, looks around and walks on. She goes off;*
ALFRED *does not notice her.* ALFRED *struggles and
overcomes the chair. He lowers it almost absent-
mindedly, looks left, then right, casually. Finally he
puts the chair beneath his arm and leaves)*

KATHLEEN   *(Offstage)*   Oh, Gawd . . . Oh . . . Nah, this
side's better . . . Oh.
   (She comes on limping, her arm in HARRY*'s.* HARRY
   carries a wicker chair under his other arm)

HARRY   Oh, look at that.

KATHLEEN   Where's the other one gone, then?

HARRY   Well, that's a damned nuisance.

KATHLEEN   Still only two. Don't know what they'll say.

HARRY   Oh, dear.

KATHLEEN   Pinch anything round here. Can't turn
your back. Gawd . . . !
   (She sinks down in the metal chair as HARRY *holds
   it for her)*

HARRY   There, now.

KATHLEEN   *(Sighing)*   Good to get off your feet . . .

HARRY   Yes, well . . .
   (He adjusts his own chair to get the sun, fussing)

KATHLEEN   Better sit on it. No good standing about.
Don't know where she's got to. Where's your friend
looking?

HARRY   Went to remedials, I believe.

KATHLEEN   Get you in there, won't let you out again.
Here . . . (HARRY *looks across at her*) He really what he
says he is?

HARRY   How do you mean?

KATHLEEN   Told us he was a doctor. Another time he
said he'd been a sanitary inspector.

HARRY   Really? Hadn't heard of that.

KATHLEEN   Go on. Know what inspecting he'll do. You
the same.

HARRY   Oh, now. Certain discriminations can be . . .

KATHLEEN   I've heard about you.

HARRY   Oh, well, you . . . er . . .

KATHLEEN   Making up things.

HARRY   Oh, well. One . . . embodies . . . of course.

KATHLEEN   What's that, then?

HARRY   Fancies . . . What's life for if you can't . . .
   (He flutters his fingers)

KATHLEEN   We've heard about that an' all.
(She imitates his action)

HARRY   Well, I'm sure you and I have, in reality, a great deal in common. After all, one looks around—what does one see?

KATHLEEN   Gawd . . .
(She groans, feeling her feet)

HARRY   A little this, a little that.

KATHLEEN   Here. Everything you know is little.

HARRY   Well . . . I . . . er . . . Yes *(Pauses)* No great role for this actor, I'm afraid. A little stage, a tiny part.

KATHLEEN   You an actor, then?

HARRY   Well, I did, as a matter of fact, at one time . . . actually, a little . . .

KATHLEEN   Here, little again. You notice?

HARRY   Oh . . . You're right.

KATHLEEN   What parts you play, then?

HARRY   Well, as a matter of fact . . . not your Hamlets, of course, your Ophelias; more the little bystander who passes by the . . .

KATHLEEN   Here. Little.

HARRY   Oh . . . yes!
(He laughs)

KATHLEEN   Play anything romantic?

HARRY   Oh, romance, now, was . . . never very far
away.

KATHLEEN   Here . . .

HARRY   One was cast, of course . . .

KATHLEEN   Think I could have been romantic.

HARRY   Oh, yes.

KATHLEEN   Had the chance . . . Got it here.

HARRY   Oh, yes . . .

KATHLEEN   Had different shoes than this . . .

HARRY   Oh, yes . . . everything, of course, provided . . .

KATHLEEN   Going to be a commotion, you ask me . . .

HARRY   Commotion?

KATHLEEN   When they get here. *(She indicates the
chairs)* Three chairs—if he brings one as well . . . He'll
have to stand.
   (She laughs)

HARRY   Could have been confiscated, you know.

KATHLEEN   Confiscated?

HARRY   Often happens. See a little pleasure and down
they come.

KATHLEEN   Here . . . little.

HARRY   Goodness . . . Yes. *(Pauses)* One of the advantages of this spot, you know, is that it catches the sun
so nicely.

KATHLEEN   What bit there is of it.

HARRY   Bit?

KATHLEEN   All that soot. Cuts it down. 'Stead of brown-
ing you, turns you black.

HARRY   Black?

KATHLEEN   All over.

HARRY   An industrial nation . . .

KATHLEEN   Gawd . . .
    (She eases her feet)

HARRY   Can't have the benefit of both. Nature as well
as . . . er . . . The one is incurred at the expense of the
other.

KATHLEEN   Your friend come in for following little
girls?

HARRY   What . . . ?

KATHLEEN   Go on—you can tell me. Cross me heart
and hope to die.

HARRY   Well . . . that's . . .

KATHLEEN   Well, then.

HARRY   I believe there were . . . er . . . certain proclivities, shall we say?

KATHLEEN   Proclivities? What's them?

HARRY   Nothing criminal, of course.

KATHLEEN   Oh, no . . .

HARRY   No prosecution . . .

KATHLEEN   Oh, no . . .

HARRY   Certain pressures, in the . . . er . . . revealed themselves.

KATHLEEN   In public?

HARRY   No. No . . . I . . . Not what I mean.

KATHLEEN   I don't know what you're saying half the time. You realize that?

HARRY   Communication is a difficult factor.

KATHLEEN   Say that again.

HARRY   I believe he was encouraged to come here for a little . . . er . . .

KATHLEEN   Here. Little.

HARRY   Oh, yes . . . As it is, very few places left now where one can be at ease.

KATHLEEN   Could go on his holidays. Seaside.

HARRY   Beaches? *(Pauses)* Crowded all the while.

KATHLEEN   Could go to the country.

HARRY   Spaces . . .

KATHLEEN   Sent me to the country once. All them trees. Worse 'n people . . . Gawd. Take them off if I thought I could get them on again. Can't understand why they don't let me have me laces. Took me belt as well. Who they think I'm going to strangle? Improved my figure, it did—the belt. Drew it in a bit.

HARRY   Oh, now, I would say, myself, the proportions were in reasonable condition.

KATHLEEN   Oh, now . . .

HARRY   Without, of course, wishing to seem immodest . . .

KATHLEEN   Get little enough encouragement in my life. Gawd! *(Pauses)* My friend, you know, was always crying.

HARRY   Oh, now.

KATHLEEN   Everywhere she went . . . cigarettes . . . No sooner in the shop, opens her mouth, and out it comes. Same on buses.

HARRY   Oh, dear, now.

KATHLEEN   Doesn't like sympathy.

HARRY   Ah, yes.

KATHLEEN   Get all I can, myself.

HARRY   Husband a bus driver, I believe.

KATHLEEN   Hers, not mine.

HARRY   Ah, yes.

KATHLEEN   Mine's a corporation employee.

HARRY   Ah, yes. One of the—

KATHLEEN   Cleans up muck. Whenever there's a pile of muck they send him to clean it up.

HARRY   I see.

KATHLEEN   You worked in a bank, then?

HARRY   Well, in a . . . er . . .

KATHLEEN   Clean job. Don't know why he doesn't get a clean job. Doorman . . . Smells awful, he does. Gets bathed one night and the next day just the same.

HARRY   Ah, yes.

KATHLEEN   Puts you off your food.

HARRY   Yes.

KATHLEEN   "They ought to fumigate you," I said.

HARRY   Yes?

KATHLEEN   Know what he says?

HARRY   Yes?

KATHLEEN   "Ought to fumigate you, my girl, and forget to switch it orf."

HARRY   Goodness!

KATHLEEN   Going to be teatime before they get here.

HARRY   *(Examining his watch)* No, no. Still a little time.

KATHLEEN   Your wife alive?

HARRY   Er . . .

KATHLEEN   Separated?

HARRY   Well, I . . .

KATHLEEN   Unsympathetic.

HARRY   Yes?

KATHLEEN   Your wife.

HARRY   Well . . . One can ask too much these days, I believe, of . . . er . . .

KATHLEEN   Met once a fortnight, wouldn't be any divorce. Ridiculous, living together. S'not human.

HARRY   No . . .

KATHLEEN   Like animals . . . Even they run off when they're not feeling like it.

HARRY   Oh, yes.

KATHLEEN   Not natural . . . One man. One woman. Who's He think He is? (HARRY *looks around*) No . . . *Him.*
      (She points up)

HARRY   Oh, yes . . .

KATHLEEN   Made Him a bachelor. Cor blimey—no wife for Him.

HARRY   No.

KATHLEEN   Saved somebody the trouble.

HARRY   Yes.

KATHLEEN   Does it all by telepathy.

HARRY   Yes.

KATHLEEN   Kids?

HARRY   What? . . . Oh . . . no.

KATHLEEN   Got married how old?

HARRY   Twenty . . . er . . .

KATHLEEN   Man shouldn't marry till he's forty. Ridiculous. Don't know what they want till then. After that,
too old to bother.

HARRY   Oh, yes.

KATHLEEN   Here . . . (ALFRED *comes in carrying the chair,
sees them and nods. Then he goes back the way he came
in. Calling after* ALFRED) Here! That's where it's gone.

HARRY   Don't believe . . .

KATHLEEN   That's Alfred.

HARRY   Yes?

KATHLEEN   Wrestler.

HARRY   Yes.

KATHLEEN   Up here.
(She taps her head)

HARRY   Oh.

KATHLEEN   Where you going when you leave here?

HARRY   Well, I . . . er . . .

KATHLEEN   Lost your job?

HARRY   Well, I . . .

KATHLEEN   Wife not have you?

HARRY   Well, I . . .

KATHLEEN   Another man.

HARRY   Oh, now . . .

KATHLEEN   Still . . . could be worse.

HARRY   Oh, yes.
(There are a few moments of silence)

KATHLEEN   What's he want with that, then? Here . . .
you were slow to ask.

HARRY   Yes . . .

KATHLEEN   You all right?

HARRY   Touch of the . . .
(He wipes his eyes and nose)

KATHLEEN   Here, couple of old crybabies, you are. Bad
as my friend.

HARRY   Yes . . . Well . . .

KATHLEEN   Shoot my brains out if I had a chance.
Gawd! *(She feels her feet)* Tried to kill myself with gas.

HARRY   Yes?

KATHLEEN   Kiddies at my sister's. Head in oven. Knock
on door. Milkman. Two weeks behind, he said. Broke
everything, I did.

HARRY   Yes?

KATHLEEN   Nearly killed him. Would, too, if I could

have got hold. Won't tap on our door, I can tell you. Not again.

HARRY   Goodness.

KATHLEEN   You all right?

HARRY   Yes . . . I . . . er . . .

KATHLEEN   Here. Hold my hand if you like.

HARRY   Oh, now.

KATHLEEN   Go on. *(She puts her hand on the table)* Not much to look at.

HARRY   Oh, now. I wouldn't say that.

KATHLEEN   Go on.

HARRY   Well, I . . .
        (He takes her hand)

KATHLEEN   Our age; know what it's all about.

HARRY   Oh, well . . . A long road, you know.

KATHLEEN   Can't get to old age fast enough for me. Sooner they put me under . . .

HARRY   Oh, now . . .

KATHLEEN   Different for a man.

HARRY   Well, I . . .

KATHLEEN   I know. Have your troubles. Still. Woman's different.

HARRY   Oh, I . . .

KATHLEEN   Wouldn't be a woman. Not again . . . Here!
(ALFRED *has entered. He passes behind them, carrying the*
chair. He glances at them and goes off) Been here years,
you know. Do the work of ten men if they set him to
it.

HARRY   I say . . .
    (He looks off)

KATHLEEN   Dunno where they've been . . . *(Calling)* Oi!
. . . Deaf as a post. Here, no need to let go . . . Think
you're shy.

HARRY   Oh, well . . .

KATHLEEN   Never mind. Too old to be disappointed.

HARRY   Oh, now . . .
    (JACK *and* MARJORIE *enter;* JACK *is carrying a*
    wicker chair)

MARJORIE   Here you are, then. Been looking for you all
over.

KATHLEEN   Been here, haven't we, all the time.
    (HARRY *stands*)

JACK   Sun still strong.

HARRY   Oh, yes.

MARJORIE   Here. Where's the other chair?

KATHLEEN   He's taken it over there.

MARJORIE   What's he doing?

KATHLEEN   Dunno. Here, sit on his knee if you want to!

MARJORIE Catch me. Who do you think I am?
(She sits)

KATHLEEN Well, no good you both standing.

JACK (*To* HARRY) No, no. After you, old man.

HARRY No, no—after you . . .

KATHLEEN Be here all day, you ask me. Here, I'll stand
. . . Gawd . . .

JACK Oh, no . . .

HARRY Ridiculous.

MARJORIE Take it in turns.

JACK Right, I'll . . . er . . .

HARRY Do, do. Go ahead.

JACK Very decent. Very.
(He sits and sighs)

MARJORIE Been carrying that around, looking for you,
he has.

KATHLEEN Been here, we have, all the time.

MARJORIE What have you been up to, then?

KATHLEEN Nothing you might mind.

MARJORIE (*To* HARRY) Want to watch her. Men all the
time.

KATHLEEN One who knows.

MARJORIE Seen it with my own eyes.

8 0

KATHLEEN   Lot more besides.

JACK   Think it might look up. Clearing . . .
(He gazes up)

HARRY   Oh. Very.
(He gazes up too)

MARJORIE   Fallen in love, she has.

JACK   Damn nuisance about that chair, what?

HARRY   Oh, very.

MARJORIE   Has to see the doctor about it, she has.

KATHLEEN   See the doctor about you, girl.

MARJORIE   Can't let no tradesman near the house. Five
kids. Milkman, window cleaner . . .

KATHLEEN   Know your trouble, don't you?

MARJORIE   Nothing s'bad as yours.

KATHLEEN   Can't go down the street without her trou-
sers wetting.

JACK   Spot more sun, see those flowers out, shouldn't
wonder.

HARRY   Oh, yes.

JACK   By jove! Farrer, isn't it?

HARRY   Say he was a champion quarter-miler.

JACK   Shouldn't be surprised. Build of an athlete.
Square shoulders.

HARRY   Deep chest.

JACK   Oh, yes.

KATHLEEN   You know what you should do with your
mouth, girl.

MARJORIE   You know what you should do with something else.

KATHLEEN   (*To* HARRY)   Take a little stroll if you don't
mind . . . Gawd's strewth . . .
(*She gets up;* HARRY *hastens to help her*)

MARJORIE   Mind she doesn't stroll you to the bushes.

KATHLEEN   Mind she doesn't splash.

MARJORIE   See the doctor about you, my girl!

KATHLEEN   See him all the time. Your trouble: not right
in the head.
(KATHLEEN *has taken* HARRY*'s arm. They go off*)

MARJORIE   Can't keep away from men.

JACK   Oh, dear.
(*He gazes after them*)

MARJORIE   Gardens.

JACK   Oh.

MARJORIE   Parks especially.

JACK   I have heard of such . . . er . . .

MARJORIE   Complaints. Used to send the police in
threes. Can't trust two, and one was never enough.

JACK My word.

MARJORIE Oh, yes.

JACK Can never tell a leopard . . .

MARJORIE What? Should see her. Spots all over.

JACK Oh, dear.

MARJORIE Never washes.

JACK One of the advantages of a late lunch, of course, is that it leaves a shorter space to tea.

MARJORIE What's your friend's name?

JACK Harry . . .

MARJORIE What's he do, then?

JACK Temporary . . . er . . . Thought a slight.

MARJORIE Get one with her all right. Have another.

JACK Oh, yes . . .

MARJORIE Don't know what we're coming to.

JACK Life . . . mystery . . .
(He gazes up. MARJORIE *watches him)*

MARJORIE What you put away for, then?

JACK Oh . . . what?

MARJORIE In here.

JACK Oh . . . Little . . .

MARJORIE Girl?

JACK Girl?

MARJORIE Girls.

JACK Girls?

MARJORIE In the street.

JACK Really?
(He looks around)

MARJORIE Here . . . What you in for?

JACK A wholly voluntary basis, I assure you.

MARJORIE Wife put you away?

JACK Oh, no. No, no. Just a moment . . . needed . . .
Thought I might . . .

MARJORIE Ever been in the padded whatsit?

JACK Don't believe . . .
(He looks around)

MARJORIE Here . . . Don't tell my friend.

JACK Oh, well . . .

MARJORIE Lie there for hours, you can.

JACK Oh, now.

MARJORIE Been here twice before.

JACK Really . . .

MARJORIE Don't tell my friend.

JACK Oh, no.

MARJORIE   Thinks it's my first.

JACK   Goodness . . .

MARJORIE   One of the regulars. Wouldn't know what to do without me.

JACK   Oh, yes. Familiar faces.

MARJORIE   Come for three months; out again. Back again at Christmas.

JACK   Oh, yes.

MARJORIE   Can't stand Christmas.

JACK   No. Well, season of festivities . . . good cheer.

MARJORIE   Most people don't talk to you in here. You noticed?

JACK   Very rare. Well . . . find someone to communicate.

MARJORIE   'Course. Privileged.

JACK   Yes?

MARJORIE   Being in the reception wing.

JACK   Oh, yes.

MARJORIE   Good as cured.

JACK   Oh, yes.

MARJORIE   Soon be out.

JACK   Oh, goodness . . . Hardly worth the trouble.

MARJORIE   No.

JACK   Home tomorrow!

MARJORIE   You been married long?

JACK   Oh, yes . . . What?

MARJORIE   You in love?

JACK   What?

MARJORIE   Your wife.

JACK   Clouds . . . This morning, my friend was remarking on the edges.

MARJORIE   Hardly worth the trouble.

JACK   Oh, yes.

MARJORIE   Going home.

JACK   Oh, well . . . one has one's . . . thought I might plant some seeds. Soil not too good, I notice . . .

MARJORIE   Tell you something?

JACK   Oh, yes.

MARJORIE   Set up here for good.

JACK   Oh, yes.

MARJORIE   Here, you listening? What you in for?

JACK   Oh . . .

MARJORIE   Here—you always crying.

8 6

JACK Light . . . eye . . .
(Wipes his eye with his handkerchief)

MARJORIE Tell you something.

JACK Yes.

MARJORIE Not leave here again.

JACK Oh, no.
(They are silent for a few moments. ALFRED *enters. He stands in back of them, leaning on the chair)*

MARJORIE You going to sit on that or something?

ALFRED What?

MARJORIE Sit?

ALFRED Dunno.

MARJORIE Give it to somebody who can, you do.

ALFRED What?

MARJORIE Give it to somebody who can.

ALFRED Yeh.

MARJORIE You know my friend?

ALFRED No.

MARJORIE This is Alfred.

JACK Oh . . . Good . . . day.
(He stands formally)

ALFRED Where you get your cane?

JACK   Oh . . . *(looks down at it)* Came with me.

ALFRED   I had a cane like that once.

JACK   Ah, yes.

ALFRED   Nicked it.

JACK   Oh, now.

MARJORIE   Had it when he came. Didn't you? Sit down.

JACK   Yes.
       (He sits)

ALFRED   Wanna fight?

JACK   No . . .

ALFRED   You?

MARJORIE   No, thanks.

ALFRED   Got sixpence?

JACK   No.

MARJORIE   Here. You seen my friend?

ALFRED   No.

MARJORIE   What you in for?

ALFRED   In what?

MARJORIE   Thinks he's at home, he does. Doesn't know his own strength—do you?

ALFRED   No.

MARJORIE   Took a bit of his brain, haven't they?

ALFRED   Yeh.

MARJORIE   Feel better?

ALFRED   Yeh.

MARJORIE   His mother's eighty-four.

ALFRED   Seventy.

MARJORIE   Thought you said she was eighty-four.

ALFRED   Seventy.

MARJORIE   Won't know his own name soon.

ALFRED   You wanna fight?

MARJORIE   Knock you down, one hand behind my back.

ALFRED   Garn.

MARJORIE   Half kill you, I will.

ALFRED   Go on.

MARJORIE   Wanna try? (*She stands.* ALFRED *backs off a couple of steps;* MARJORIE *sits*) Take that chair off you, you don't look out.

JACK   Slight breeze. Takes the heat off the sun.

MARJORIE   Wanna jump on him if he bullies you.

JACK   Oh, yes.

MARJORIE   (*To* ALFRED)   What you looking at, then?

ALFRED   Sky.
      (*He looks up*)

MARJORIE   They'll lock you up if you don't look out. How old's your father?

ALFRED   Twenty-two.

MARJORIE   Older than him, are you?

ALFRED   Yeh.

MARJORIE   Older than his dad, he is. Don't know where that leaves him.

JACK   Hasn't been born, I shouldn't wonder.

MARJORIE   No! *(Laughs)* Hasn't been born, he shouldn't wonder . . . Painted rude letters in the road.

ALFRED   Didn't.

MARJORIE   Did.

ALFRED   Didn't.

MARJORIE   Did. Right in the town center. Took them three weeks to scrub it off.

ALFRED   Two.

MARJORIE   Three.

ALFRED   Two.

MARJORIE   Three. Apprentice painter and decorator. Didn't know what he was going to decorate. (*To* ALFRED) They'll apprentice you no more. (*To* JACK) Doesn't know his own strength, he doesn't.

JACK   *(Looking around)*   Wonder where . . .

MARJORIE   Send the police out for them, they will . . .

JACK   Clouds . . .
    (He looks up)

MARJORIE   Seen it all, I have. Rape, intercourse. Physi-
    cal pleasure.

JACK   I had a cousin once . . .

MARJORIE   Here, you got a big family, haven't you?

JACK   Seven brothers and sisters. Spreads around, you
    know.

MARJORIE   Here, you was an only child last week.

JACK   A niece of mine—I say niece . . . she was only . . .

MARJORIE   What you do it for?

JACK   Oh, now . . .

MARJORIE   *(To* ALFRED*)*   Wanna watch him. Trained as
    a doctor, he has.

JACK   Wonder where . . .
    (He gazes around)

MARJORIE   *(To* ALFRED*)*   What you paint in the road?

ALFRED   Nothing.

MARJORIE   Must have painted something. Can't paint
    nothing. Must have painted something or they
    couldn't have rubbed it off.

ALFRED   Paint you, if you don't watch out.

MARJORIE   I'll knock your head off.

ALFRED   Won't.

MARJORIE   Will.

ALFRED   Won't.

MARJORIE   Will.

ALFRED   Won't.

MARJORIE   What you doing with that chair?

ALFRED   Nothing.
(He spins it beneath his hand)

MARJORIE   Faster than a rocket, he is. Wanna watch him
. . . Where you going?
(JACK *has stood up*)

JACK   Thought I might . . . Oh . . .
(HARRY *and* KATHLEEN *have entered from the other
side;* KATHLEEN *is leaning on* HARRY*'s arm*)

KATHLEEN   Gawd . . . they're coming off. I'll have nothing left . . . Oh . . .
(HARRY *helps her to the chair*)

MARJORIE   Here, where you been?

KATHLEEN   There and back.

MARJORIE   Know where you been, my girl.

KATHLEEN   Don't.

HARRY   Canteen. We've . . .

KATHLEEN   Don't tell her. Nose ten miles long, she
has. Trip over it one day, she will. What's he doing?
(She points to ALFRED*)*

MARJORIE   Won't give up his chair, he won't.

HARRY   Still got three, what?

JACK   Yes . . . what. Clouds . . .

HARRY   Ah . . . Rain.

JACK   Shouldn't wonder.

MARJORIE   Here. Put that chair down. (ALFRED *still
stands there.* MARJORIE *stands.* ALFRED *releases the chair
quickly.* MARJORIE *turns to face* JACK) You get it.

JACK   Er . . . right.
(He goes and gets the chair. ALFRED *doesn't move)*

MARJORIE   One each, then.

HARRY   Yes . . .

MARJORIE   Well . . .
(She motions to them to sit)

KATHLEEN   Gawd . . .
(Holds her feet)

MARJORIE   Had a job once.

KATHLEEN   Gawd.

MARJORIE   Packing tins of food.

KATHLEEN   (*To* ALFRED)   What you looking at?

ALFRED   Nothing.

MARJORIE   Pull your skirt down, girl.

KATHLEEN   Got nothing up mine ain't got up yours.

MARJORIE   Put them in cardboard boxes.

JACK   Really? I had a . . .

MARJORIE   Done by machine now.

KATHLEEN   Nothing left for you to do, my girl. That's your trouble.

MARJORIE   'Tis.

KATHLEEN   Cries everywhere, she does.

HARRY   Oh. One has one's . . .

KATHLEEN   Specially at Christmas. Cries at Christmas. Boxing Day. Sometimes to New Year.

JACK   Oh, well, one . . .

KATHLEEN   (*Indicating* ALFRED) What's he doing, then?

MARJORIE   Waiting to be born, he is.

KATHLEEN   What?

MARJORIE   Eight o'clock tomorrow morning. Better be there. (*Laughs; to* ALFRED) You better be there.

ALFRED   Yeh.

MARJORIE   Late for his own birthday, he is. (*To* ALFRED) Never catch up, you won't.

HARRY   (*Holding out his hand, he inspects it*) Thought I . . . No.

9 4

JACK   Could be.
        (He looks up)

HARRY   Lucky so far.

JACK   Oh, yes.

HARRY   Possibility . . .
        (He looks up)

JACK   By jove . . .

MARJORIE   One thing you can say about this place—

KATHLEEN   Yes.

MARJORIE   S'not like home.

KATHLEEN   Thank Gawd.

MARJORIE   *(To* ALFRED*)* What you want?

ALFRED   Nothing.

KATHLEEN   Give you nothing if you come here . . .
        What you staring at?

ALFRED   Nothing.

MARJORIE   Taken off a bit of his brain, they have.

KATHLEEN   *(To* ALFRED*)* Where they put it, then?

MARJORIE   Thrown it in the dustbin.

KATHLEEN   Could have done with that. *(Laughs)* Didn't
        cut a bit of something else off, did they?

MARJORIE   You know what your trouble is, my girl.

JACK   Time for tea, I shouldn't wonder.
(He stands)

HARRY   Yes. Well . . . let me see. Very nearly.

JACK   Stretch the old legs . . .

HARRY   Oh, yes.

MARJORIE   Not your legs need stretching, ask me.

JACK   Ah, well . . . Trim.
(He bends his arms and stretches)

MARJORIE   Fancies himself, he does.

KATHLEEN   Don't blame him.

MARJORIE   Watch yourself, my girl.

KATHLEEN   No harm come from trying.

MARJORIE   Good job your feet like they are, ask me.

KATHLEEN   Have them off in the morning. Not stand this much longer.

MARJORIE   Slow her down; know what they're doing.

KATHLEEN   Know what she is?

JACK   Well, I . . .

KATHLEEN   P.O.

JACK   P.O.

KATHLEEN   Persistent Offender.

MARJORIE   Ain't no such thing.

ACT TWO

KATHLEEN Is.

MARJORIE Isn't.

KATHLEEN Heard it in the office. Off Doctor ... what's-his-name.

MARJORIE Never heard of that doctor, I haven't. Must be a new one, must that. Doctor what's-his-name is a new one on me.

KATHLEEN I know what I heard.

MARJORIE Here, what's he crying about?
(HARRY *is drying his eyes*)

KATHLEEN Always crying, one of these two.

MARJORIE Call them the water babies, you ask me.
(ALFRED *gazes woodenly towards them*)

KATHLEEN My dad was always crying.

MARJORIE Yeh?

KATHLEEN Drank too much. Came out of his eyes.

MARJORIE Ooh!
(*She laughs, covering her mouth*)

KATHLEEN Here, what's the matter with you, Harry?

HARRY Oh, just a ... er ...

JACK Could have sworn ...
(*He holds out his hand and looks up*)

KATHLEEN S'not rain. S'him. Splashing it all over, he is.

JACK There, now ...

97

MARJORIE   Here. Look at him: thinks it's raining.

KATHLEEN   (*To* JACK)   Here. Your friend . . .
(JACK *breathes deeply, doing fresh air exercises*)

JACK   Freshening.

MARJORIE   I don't know. What they come out for?

KATHLEEN   Crying all over, they are.

MARJORIE   (*To* JACK)   You going to help your friend,
then, are you?

JACK   Oh, comes and goes . . .

KATHLEEN   (*To* HARRY)   Wanna hold my hand?
(HARRY *remains silent*)

MARJORIE   Not seen so many tears. Haven't.

KATHLEEN   Not since Christmas.

MARJORIE   Not since Christmas, girl.

KATHLEEN   Ooooh!

MARJORIE   (*To* JACK)   You all right? (JACK *does not an-
swer, but stands stiffly turned away, looking off*) Think
you and I better be on our way, girl.

KATHLEEN   Think we had.

MARJORIE   Try and make something. What you get for
it?

KATHLEEN   Get nothing if you don't try, girl.

MARJORIE   No.

ACT TWO

KATHLEEN   Get nothing if you do, either.

MARJORIE   Ooooh! *(Laughs, covering her mouth; stands)* Don't slow you down, do they?
(She points to KATHLEEN'*s shoes)*

KATHLEEN   Get my laces back or else, girl . . . Oh! *(She winces and gets up, then turns to* ALFRED*)* What you staring at?

ALFRED   Nothing.

KATHLEEN   Be dead this time tomorrow.

MARJORIE   No complaints then, my girl.

KATHLEEN   Not too soon for me.

MARJORIE   Going to say goodbye to your boyfriend?

KATHLEEN   Dunno that he wants to know . . .

MARJORIE   Give you a hand, girl?
(She starts to leave)

KATHLEEN   Can't move without.

MARJORIE   Here . . . on our way.

KATHLEEN   Gawd.

MARJORIE   Not stop here again.

KATHLEEN   Better get out of here, girl . . . Gawd! Go mad here, you don't watch out.
(Groaning, KATHLEEN *is led off by* MARJORIE. *There is a pause, then* ALFRED *comes up to them. He holds the table, waits, then lifts it, raising it above his head. He turns and walks off)*

JACK   By jove. (HARRY *stirs*) Freshening . . . Surprised
if it doesn't blow over by tomorrow.

HARRY   Oh, yes . . .

JACK   Saw Harrison yesterday.

HARRY   Yes?

JACK   Congestion.

HARRY   Soot.

JACK   Really?

HARRY   Oh, yes.
(He dries his eyes)

JACK   Shouldn't wonder if wind veers. Northwest.

HARRY   East.

JACK   Really? Higher ground, of course, one notices.

HARRY   Found the . . . er . . .
(He gestures after MARJORIE *and* KATHLEEN*)*

JACK   Oh, yes.

HARRY   Extraordinary.

JACK   'Straordinary.

HARRY   Get used to it after a while.

JACK   Oh, yes . . . I have a sister-in-law, for example,
who wears dark glasses.

HARRY   Really?

JACK   Each evening, before she goes to bed.

HARRY   Really.

JACK   Following morning, takes them off.

HARRY   Extraordinary.

JACK   Sunshine—never wears them.

HARRY   Well . . . I . . . *(Finally wipes his eyes and puts his handkerchief away)* Extraordinary.

JACK   The older one grows, of course . . . the more one takes into account other people's foibles.

HARRY   Oh, yes.

JACK   If a person can't be what they are, what's the purpose of being anything at all?

HARRY   Oh, absolutely.
   (ALFRED *has returned. He picks up one of the metalwork chairs, turns it one way then another, gazes at them, then slowly carries it off*)

JACK   I suppose in the Army, of course, one becomes quite used to foibles.

HARRY   Oh, yes.

JACK   Navy, too, I shouldn't wonder.

HARRY   Oh, yes.

JACK   A relative of mine rose to lieutenant-commander in a seagoing corvette.

HARRY   My word.

JACK   In the blood.

HARRY   Bound to be.

JACK   Oh, yes. Without the sea—well, hate to think.

HARRY   Oh, yes.

JACK   At no point is one more than seventy-five miles from the sea.

HARRY   Really?

JACK   That is the nature of this little island.

HARRY   Extraordinary, when you think.

JACK   When you think what came from it.

HARRY   Oh, yes.

JACK   Radar.

HARRY   Oh, yes.

JACK   Jet propulsion.

HARRY   My word.

JACK   Television.

HARRY   Oh . . .

JACK   Steam engine.

HARRY   Goodness.

JACK   Empire the like of which no one has ever seen.

HARRY   No. My word.

JACK   Light of the world.

HARRY   Oh, yes.

JACK   Penicillin.

HARRY   Penicillin.

JACK   Darwin.

HARRY   Darwin.

JACK   Newton.

HARRY   Newton.

JACK   Milton.

HARRY   My word.

JACK   Sir Walter Raleigh.

HARRY   Goodness. Sir . . .

JACK   Lost his head.

HARRY   Oh, yes.

JACK   This little island.

HARRY   Shan't see its like.

JACK   Oh, no.

HARRY   The sun has set.

JACK   Couple of hours . . .

HARRY   What?

JACK   One of the strange things, of course, about this
place . . .

HARRY   Oh, yes.

JACK   . . . is its size.

HARRY   Yes.

JACK   Never meet the same people two days running.

HARRY   No.

JACK   Can't find room, of course.

HARRY   No.

JACK   See them at the gates.

HARRY   Oh, my word.

JACK   Of an evening, looking in. Unfortunately, the
money isn't there.

HARRY   No.

JACK   Exchequer. Diverting wealth to the proper . . .

HARRY   Oh, yes.

JACK   Witness: one metalwork table, two metalwork
chairs; two thousand people.

HARRY   My word, yes.

JACK   While overhead . . .

HARRY   Oh, yes . . .
(They both gaze up. ALFRED *comes in; he picks up the
remaining metalwork chair)*

ALFRED   You finished?

JACK   What?

ALFRED   Take them back.
(*He indicates their two wicker chairs*)

HARRY   Oh, yes . . .

ALFRED   Don't take them back; get into trouble.

JACK   Oh, my word. (ALFRED, *watching them, lifts the metal chair with one hand, holding its legs, and demonstrates his strength. They watch in silence.* ALFRED *lifts the chair above his head; then, still watching them, he turns and goes*) Shadows.

HARRY   Yes.

JACK   Another day.

HARRY   Ah, yes.

JACK   Brother-in-law I had was an artist.

HARRY   Really?

JACK   Would have appreciated those flowers. Light fading . . . Clouds.

HARRY   Wonderful thing.

JACK   Oh, yes.

HARRY   Would have liked to have been an artist myself —musician.

JACK   Really?

HARRY   Flute.

JACK   Beautiful instrument.

HARRY   Oh, yes. *(They gaze at the view)* Shadows.

JACK   Choose any card . . .
       (He holds the pack out from his pocket)

HARRY   Any?

JACK   Any one . . .

HARRY   *(Taking one)* Yes . . . !

JACK   Eight of diamonds.

HARRY   My word!

JACK   Right?

HARRY   Absolutely.

JACK   Intended to show the ladies.

HARRY   Another day.

JACK   Oh, yes.
       (JACK *re-shuffles the cards and holds them out)*

HARRY   Again?

JACK   Any one.

HARRY   Er . . .

JACK   Three of spades.

HARRY   Two of hearts.

JACK   What?
       (He inspects the cards briefly, then puts them away)

HARRY   Amazing thing, of course, is the . . . er . . .

JACK   Oh, yes.

HARRY   Still prevails.

JACK   Oh, my goodness.

HARRY   Hendricks, I find, is a . . .

JACK   Oh, yes.

HARRY   Mustache . . . eyebrows.

JACK   Divorced.

HARRY   Oh, yes.

JACK   Moral fiber. Set to a task, never complete it. Find some way to back out.

HARRY   Oh, yes.

JACK   The sea is an extraordinary . . .

HARRY   Oh, yes.

JACK   Cousin of mine.

HARRY   See the church.
      (They gaze off)

JACK   Shouldn't wonder—He's disappointed.
      (He looks up)

HARRY   Oh, yes.

JACK   Heartbreak.

HARRY   Oh, yes.

JACK   Same mistake . . . Won't make it twice.

HARRY   Oh, no.

JACK   Once over. Never again.
(ALFRED *has entered*)

ALFRED   You finished?

JACK   Well, I . . . er . . .

ALFRED   Take 'em back.

JACK   Oh, well. That's very . . . (ALFRED *grasps the two wicker chairs, glances at* JACK *and* HARRY, *then picks up both the chairs. Glances at* JACK *and* HARRY *again, holding the chairs. Takes them off*) What I . . . er . . . yes.
(HARRY *has begun to weep.* JACK *gazes off. A moment later* JACK *also wipes his eyes. After a while the light slowly fades*)

Curtain

DAVID STOREY was born in 1933, the third son of a coal miner, in Yorkshire, England. He gained a place in the Honours Geography School at Reading University, but decided at the last minute to study art. In order to provide for his art education, he was a professional rugby player for four seasons. He graduated in Painting from the Slade School of Fine Arts, London, and exhibited his works with a group of other Yorkshire artists. Then came four years of teaching in secondary schools in London's East End.

Mr. Storey began his writing career as a novelist. His novel *This Sporting Life* won the Macmillan Fiction Award for 1960 in the United States, and was made into a film in 1963. Two other novels, *Flight into Camden* and *Radcliffe*, followed. His first two plays, *The Restoration of Arnold Middleton* (1966) and *In Celebration* (1968) were very successful on the London stage. In 1970, Mr. Storey's two new plays, *The Contractor* and *Home*, were produced at the Royal Court Theatre, the innovative theater company that has introduced many fine British playwrights. Both plays attracted much attention, and because of their popularity were transferred to the West End for extended runs. *Home*, starring Sir John Gielgud and Sir Ralph Richardson, subsequently opened on Broadway, where it received high critical acclaim.

David Storey has recently completed a fifth play, and is now at work on a novel. He is married and lives in London with his wife and four children.